Cornerstones of Freedom

U.S. Olympians

Zachary Kent

CHILDRENS PRESS ®

CHICAGO

Library of Congress Cataloging-in-Publication Data

Kent, Zachary.
U.S. Olympians / by Zachary Kent.

   p. cm. — (Cornerstones of freedom)
  Summary: Highlights dramatic moments in the history
of the United States's participation in the Olympic
games.
  ISBN 0-516-06659-5
  1. Olympics—Juvenile literature. 2. Winter Olympics
—Juvenile literature. [1. Olympics.] I. Title. II. Series.
GV721.5.K45   1992
973.04973—dc20   92-4812
                       CIP
                       AC

Seventy thousand eager spectators jammed the giant new stadium in Athens, Greece, on April 6, 1896. The cheering crowd waved bright flags as 311 amateur athletes from 13 different nations marched onto the field. They roared even more loudly when King George I rose from his seat. "I hereby proclaim," the Greek king announced, "the opening of the First International Olympic Games."

On the grassy field, American triple-jumper James B. Connolly felt almost dazed. For Connolly, just reaching the Games had been a challenging adventure. Harvard University officials had refused to grant the twenty-seven-year-old student a leave of absence so that he could compete in the Games. Stubbornly, Connolly packed his bags and dropped out of Harvard. Paying his own way, he joined thirteen other American athletes sailing for Europe. During the sixteen-day boat trip to Naples, Italy, Connolly's wallet was stolen. Then, when the Americans finally arrived in Italy, Connolly nearly missed the cross-country train. Teammates hauled him aboard the moving railroad car through an open window. Another

James Connolly

boat ride carried the Americans from Italy to Greece. When Connolly at last arrived in Athens, exhausted, he thought he had twelve days to rest before the triple-jump competition.

The blaring noise of a brass band awakened the Americans the next morning. "Our eyes almost popped out," team member Robert Garrett later declared. "That big parade outside was the start of the Olympic ceremonies. . . . Somebody back home had read the calendar wrong." The athletes hadn't known that Greece, at that time, used a different calender than the United States. Connolly rushed to the stadium with his teammates. After the opening ceremonies, he found his way to the pit for the triple-jump competition. On his first turn, Connolly galloped down the runway. At the take-off board, he hopped, hopped, and then jumped forward. "I seemed to soar, and as I landed in the pit a tremendous cheer went up. . . . By and by, I took my second try. Another roar went up."

"There's nobody within a yard of you," an English jumper soon told Connolly. Sure enough, with an effort of nearly 45 feet, he beat his closest rival by more than 3 feet. Actually, under today's rules, Connolly would have been disqualified, since he performed two hops and a jump instead of the correct sequence of hop, step, and jump. But at the time, Connolly's style was considered acceptable.

The first modern Olympic Games were held in 1896 in Athens, Greece.

In spite of his many troubles, a grinning James B. Connolly became the first modern Olympic champion. Since that time, all of America's Olympic athletes have shown a special brand of courage. Every four years, their spirit brings drama and excitement to the Olympic Games, the most important sports competition in the world.

The first recorded Olympics were held in the Greek city of Olympia in 776 B.C. (though Olympic games had probably been occurring for about five hundred years by that time). Originally, there was only one event: a sprint race. That year, it was won by a young runner named Coroebus, who dashed the length of the

The Olympic motto, which translates: "swifter, higher, stronger"

At ancient Olympic contests, the winners were crowned with a wreath of wild olive leaves.

Olympic stadium to become the first recorded Olympic champion. Over the next thousand years, the Greeks added other events to their Olympic contests. Breathing hard, some athletes ran side by side in foot races. Others jumped for distance, hurled the discus, or heaved the long, pointed javelin. Crowds watched thrilling chariot races and saw muscled wrestlers locked in combat. The winner of each contest was honored by having a wreath of olive leaves placed upon his head.

In A.D. 393, Roman Emperor Theodosius halted the Olympic competitions. For the next fifteen hundred years, the Olympics existed as only a fading memory.

In the late 1800s, however, a certain Frenchman became very interested in the glory of the ancient Olympics. Baron Pierre de Coubertin believed that sports and sportsmanship should be included in every student's education. He dreamed of bringing together amateur athletes from all over the world to compete in a revival of the Olympic Games. Like the ancient Games, the modern Games would be held every four years. Full of enthusiasm, Coubertin organized the first modern Olympics, to be held in Athens, Greece, in 1896.

The volunteer American team came very close to missing those Games. James B. Connolly and his thirteen weary teammates soon amazed everyone, however. In all, the Americans won eleven first-place medals, more than any other nation.

The 1896 Athens Olympics were a great success. But over the next few years, Baron de Coubertin worried about the future of the modern Olympic Games. He felt that the Games weren't being given the attention they deserved. In 1904, for example, the United States staged the Olympics as merely a sideshow to its World's Fair in St. Louis. Very few foreign nations even bothered to send athletic teams. "The Olympics

Baron Pierre de Coubertin

A street decoration from the 1896 Olympics

didn't amount to much then," 800-meter runner Emil Breitkreutz later recalled. Of the Olympic events that visitors bothered to watch in 1904, the marathon was the one that probably received the most attention.

The marathon race has an interesting origin. In 490 B.C., a Greek messenger named Pheidippedes had hurried from the Plains of Marathon to Athens. He carried important news of Greek victory over an army of invading Persians. With bloody feet and heaving lungs, Pheidippedes raced the distance of roughly twenty-five miles. "Rejoice—we conquer!" he cried out in the Athens marketplace before falling to the ground, dead. To honor that legend, athletes have run a marathon at every modern Olympics.

The three leading runners of the 1904 Olympic marathon in St Louis

Thomas Hicks (third from left), the winner of the 1904 Olympic marathon

On a broiling-hot August day in 1904, the St. Louis marathon runners began their race. Through city streets and past country pastures, they jogged the long, winding course. "The roads were so lined with vehicles," declared one witness, "that the runners had to constantly dodge the horses and wagons." New Yorker Fred Lorz—looking remarkably fresh—entered the stadium and crossed the finish line far ahead of anyone else. After accepting the winner's trophy, he laughingly admitted that he had ridden part of the way by automobile. Staggering into the stadium, Boston runner Thomas Hicks soon claimed the victory honestly.

A weight lifter at the 1904 Games

The 1908 Olympics were held in London, England. King Edward VII wished to watch the start of the marathon from his home, so it was arranged for the runners to start at Windsor Castle and race to the Olympic Stadium. That distance of exactly 26 miles and 385 yards is the official marathon length today.

By 1908, the Olympics included more than one hundred events and attracted fans and athletes from all over the world. Baron de Coubertin's modern Olympics have grown bigger and better with each Olympiad. Since 1924, Winter Games as well as Summer Games have been part of the Olympic tradition.

The Winter Olympics, first held in 1924, include such cold-weather sports as figure skating (left) and skiing (right).

The gold-medal-winning 1988 U.S. Olympic women's basketball team

Track and field, basketball, boxing, canoeing, cycling, horsemanship, fencing, gymnastics, rowing, shooting, soccer, swimming, volleyball, water polo, weight lifting, wrestling, and yachting are some of the sports found at the Summer Games. The Winter Games include such cold-weather sports as bobsledding, figure skating, ice hockey, skiing, and speed skating.

Citius, Altius, Fortius, urges the Olympic motto. The meaning of these Latin words is "Swifter, Higher, Stronger." Since the very beginning, many American Olympic athletes have achieved these goals.

Jim Thorpe performing two of the ten events of the decathlon: the shot put (right) and the long jump (below)

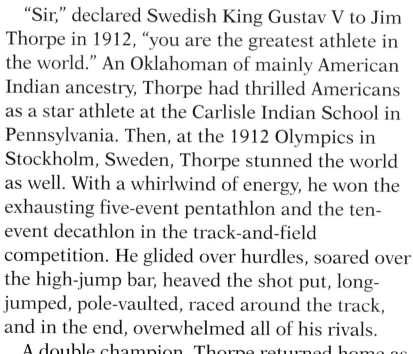

"Sir," declared Swedish King Gustav V to Jim Thorpe in 1912, "you are the greatest athlete in the world." An Oklahoman of mainly American Indian ancestry, Thorpe had thrilled Americans as a star athlete at the Carlisle Indian School in Pennsylvania. Then, at the 1912 Olympics in Stockholm, Sweden, Thorpe stunned the world as well. With a whirlwind of energy, he won the exhausting five-event pentathlon and the ten-event decathlon in the track-and-field competition. He glided over hurdles, soared over the high-jump bar, heaved the shot put, long-jumped, pole-vaulted, raced around the track, and in the end, overwhelmed all of his rivals.

A double champion, Thorpe returned home as America's first true sports hero. But years of bitterness soon followed. A reporter discovered that Thorpe had earned a few dollars a week playing minor-league baseball one summer. Technically, this made him a professional rather than amateur athlete—and only amateur athletes were allowed in the Olympics. The International Olympic Committee (IOC) stripped Thorpe of his gold medals. Though most people felt that the punishment was too harsh, the IOC held firm. Thorpe himself was deeply crushed. He went on to become a professional baseball and football star, but led a troubled life, and died nearly penniless in 1953. In 1982, the IOC finally pardoned the deserving Olympian and returned his name to the record books.

A Hawaiian named Duke Kahanamoku started off America's winning tradition in Olympic swimming events. At Stockholm in 1912,

The 1912 U.S. Olympic men's swim team

Duke Kahanamoku

Kahanamoku surprised spectators with his flutter kick and Hawaiian-crawl swimming style. Diving into the water, he easily won the 100-meter freestyle race. Eight years later, at the 1920 Antwerp Olympics, he won a second gold medal in the same event.

At the 1924 Paris Olympics, Kahanamoku had to settle for the second-place silver medal in the 100-meter freestyle. A tall, lanky nineteen-year-old from Chicago named Johnny Weissmuller glided ahead to victory. Altogether, Weissmuller's record-breaking swimming earned him three gold medals in Paris, and two more in Amsterdam in 1928. A Hollywood movie studio eventually signed the handsome swimmer to play the role of Tarzan. On the silver screen,

The start of the 400-meter freestyle swimming race at the 1932 Los Angeles Games

Swimmers Johnny Weissmuller (left) and Buster Crabbe (above, on left) both became movie stars after winning gold medals in the Olympics.

Weissmuller swung on jungle vines and uttered such famous lines as "Me Tarzan—you Jane."

Hollywood discovered another swimming champion at the 1932 Olympics in Los Angeles. After splashing to first-place victory in the 400-meter freestyle event, Clarence "Buster" Crabbe became a movie star, playing the roles of comic-book heroes Flash Gordon and Buck Rogers.

Olympic athletes enjoyed something new at the 1932 Los Angeles Games. On 250 acres of land, workers hammered together the first Olympic Village. The village included rows of comfortable two-room houses, forty kitchens, a hospital, a library, a post office, and even a barbershop. At

The first Olynpic Village was built for the 1932 Los Angeles Games.

previous Olympics, the national teams had lived apart and trained secretly. At this marvelous Olympic Village, however, thirteen hundred male athletes from thirty-seven nations mingled together, making friends easily and learning about foreign cultures.

Another marvel at Los Angeles in 1932 was an eighteen-year-old, five-foot-four-inch Texan named Mildred "Babe" Didrikson. Earlier that summer, Didrikson had won the U.S. women's track-and-field national team championship single-handedly. The second-place team of twenty-two women had been no match for the sensational athlete.

At the Los Angeles Games, Didrikson set

Olympic track-and-field star Babe Didrikson (above, first from right) went on to become a champion golfer (below).

stunning world records while winning the 80-meter hurdles and the javelin throw. She might have won the high-jump contest, too, but had to settle for the silver medal after officials decided that the "dive-and-roll" style of her last jump was illegal. The crowds loved the outspoken young Texan. Marveling at Didrikson's skill in swimming, riding, rowing, tennis, basketball, baseball, and other sports, a reporter asked the athlete, "Is there anything at all you don't play?"

"Yeah," she answered. "Dolls."

After her Olympic career, "Babe the Unbeatable" went on to become a champion golfer, winning every major title on the professional tour.

The 1936 Berlin Games introduced the tradition of lighting the Olympic flame (below) with a torch relayed from Olympia, Greece (above).

Ranks of parading German soldiers marched the goose step through Berlin in 1936. That year, German dictator Adolf Hitler was determined to make the Berlin Summer Olympics a showcase for his Nazi political party. The 1936 Olympics are also remembered for being the first Games at which a runner carried a torch into the stadium on opening day. The torch had been lit in Olympia, Greece, and relayed across Europe by nearly three thousand athletes, each of whom carried the torch for one kilometer. The last runner, arriving at the stadium to the cheers of a hundred thousand spectators, ran a final lap around the track, then used the torch to ignite a flame that would burn throughout the Games.

Jesse Owens's unparalleled performance at the 1936 Berlin Games shattered the Nazi myth of German athletic superiority.

The torch relay has been part of the Olympic tradition ever since.

Hitler's Nazi propaganda claimed that the Germans were a pure-blooded master race that was better than Jews, blacks, and many other groups. The 1936 U.S. track-and-field team included ten African Americans, and they were determined to prove Hitler wrong. The most promising athlete among them was twenty-two-year-old James "Jesse" Owens. In the 100-meter dash, while Hitler watched unhappily from the stands, Owens charged forward with legs churning and sprinted first across the finish line. The next day, Owens soared to victory in the long-jump event with a record leap of 26 feet, 5-1/2 inches. On his third day of competition,

Owens streaked down the track to win the 200-meter race. He further amazed spectators when, a few days later, he earned a fourth gold medal as a member of the world-record-breaking 4 x 100-meter relay team. Excited sportswriters called Jesse Owens the greatest track-and-field athlete of the century. His African-American teammates joined him in winning a total of eight gold medals, three silver medals, and two bronze medals. Together they shattered the Nazi myth of German athletic superiority.

Because of World War II, no Olympic Games were held in 1940 and 1944. Three years after the defeat of Germany and Japan, hopeful athletes gathered in London, England, for the 1948 Olympics. Few people thought that a seventeen-year-old Californian named Bob Mathias had much chance to win the grueling decathlon.

Bob Mathias hurls the discus (left) and clears the high-jump bar (right) on his way to winning the decathlon in 1948.

Mathias had just graduated from high school and had been training for the decathlon for only two months. Yet in the London rain, Mathias surpassed his rivals as he skimmed over hurdles, hurled the discus, and raced on the muddy track. At the end of two days, the exhausted teenager raised his arms in triumph as he became the youngest decathlon winner in Olympic history.

At the 1952 Olympics in Helsinki, Finland, Mathias won his second decathlon. That year, the shadow of politics once more loomed over the Games. For the first time, the Soviet Union entered the competition. The Soviets collected more Olympic medals than the United States and

The U.S. hockey team celebrates its victory over the Soviets in 1980.

bragged that their communist system was better than American democracy.

The strong political rivalry between the U.S.A. and the U.S.S.R. lasted through many Olympic Games. A ragtag U.S. hockey team upset the favored U.S.S.R. team to win the gold at the 1980 Winter Games at Lake Placid, New York. Across America, proud citizens chanted "U.S.A.!" in wild celebration. To protest the 1979 Soviet invasion of Afghanistan, U.S. president Jimmy Carter organized a sixty-six-nation boycott of the 1980 Summer Olympics in Moscow. In 1984, the Soviet Union retaliated by organizing a boycott of its own. The U.S.S.R. and fourteen other nations refused to take part in the Los Angeles Games that summer.

While on the victory stand in 1968, Tommie Smith and John Carlos raised black-gloved fists to protest racial discrimination in the United States.

In 1968, black American athletes had used their Olympic success as an opportunity to make a social protest. At the Summer Games in Mexico City, Tommie Smith and John Carlos won gold and bronze medals in the 200-meter dash. On the victory stand, while "The Star-Spangled Banner" played, Smith and Carlos lowered their heads and raised black-gloved fists to protest racial discrimination in the United States.

Tragedy shocked the world at the 1972 Munich Olympics. On September 5, 1972, a group of armed Arab terrorists snuck into the Olympic

Flags hang at half-mast after the tragedy in Munich

Village, murdered two Israeli athletes, and took nine other Israelis hostage. Later, in a violent airport shoot-out, the nine hostages were killed, along with five terrorists and a German policeman. After the horrible massacre, flags hung at half-mast. Stunned and weeping athletes dedicated the rest of the Munich Games to the memory of the slain Israelis.

In spite of tragedy and politics, the Olympic Games endure. The triumphs of America's athletes remain a constant source of national pride. Boxing greats Floyd Patterson, Muhammad Ali, Joe Frazier, George Foreman, and "Sugar" Ray Leonard, for example, all first gained fame winning gold in the Olympics.

Such boxing greats as Floyd Patterson (below, ducking punch) and Muhammad Ali (right, on first-place victory stand) first gained fame as Olympic champions.

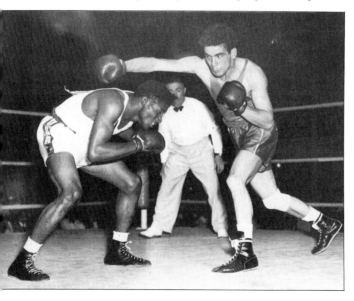

At the 1960 Rome Olympics, French reporters nicknamed U.S. sprinter Wilma Rudolph "The Gazelle." As a young child in Tennessee, Rudolph had suffered an illness that left her with a paralyzed left leg. Over the years, however, she gradually strengthened her legs by running and playing basketball with her brothers. By the time she was sixteen, she had developed into a star runner and had qualified for the U.S. Olympic team. In Rome, twenty-year-old Wilma exploded from the starting blocks and won both the 100-meter and the 200-meter sprints. Then, in the 400-meter relay, she dashed ahead on the last lap to score a third victory for the U.S. team.

Wilma Rudolph

No American had ever won the Olympic 10,000-meter run. But at the 1964 Tokyo Olympics, twenty-six-year-old Billy Mills, a part Sioux Indian, upset his rivals with an incredible effort. "I knew I had a chance if I could stay with the leaders," he exclaimed afterward. Surging ahead, Mills won the long distance race in Olympic-record time.

Four years later, another American track-and-field star surprised the world. At the 1968 Olympics in Mexico City, long-jumper Bob Beamon sprang down the runway and launched himself into space. He sailed through the air at an unbelievable height, landing almost beyond the far edge of the pit. "Tell me I'm not dreaming!" he yelled when the judges announced

Billy Mills

25

Patricia McCormick

Mark Spitz

his distance. His incredible jump of 29 feet 2-1/2 inches beat the old world record by 16 inches. None of the other competitors came even close to Beamon's remarkable jump.

For lasting strength, few athletes have been able to match the career of U.S. discus thrower Al Oerter. "I get fired up for the Olympics," Oerter once declared. In Melbourne, Australia, in 1956; Rome, Italy, in 1960; and Tokyo, Japan, in 1964; Oerter snatched victory. In Mexico City in 1968, Oerter once more gathered his energy. Hurling the discus farther than anyone else, he won his fourth and final Olympic gold medal.

Graceful American diver Patricia McCormick scored impressive Olympic victories in both the platform and springboard diving events in 1952 and again in 1956. Plunging into the water in 1984 and 1988, Greg Louganis equaled McCormick's "double-double" success in the men's diving competitions. Perhaps the king of Olympic water sports, however, is U.S. swimmer Mark Spitz. At Munich in 1972, the twenty-two-year-old poured on the power, claiming victory in such races as the 200-meter butterfly, 100-meter freestyle, and 200-meter freestyle, all in new world-record times. By the end of the Games, Spitz wore an astonishing seven Olympic gold medals around his neck.

The United States has had its share of Winter Olympics stars as well. Figure skater Dick Button, who won gold medals in 1948 and 1952, invented spins and backward leaps that were still used to win the gold by Scott Hamilton in 1984 and Brian Boitano in 1988. "How do you like my new little necklace?" asked nineteen-year-old Peggy Fleming, showing off her 1968 gold medal for women's figure skating. Eight years later, figure-skater Dorothy Hamill stole the hearts of Americans when she won the gold at Montreal. Soon, little girls all over America were imitating Hamill's "wedge" haircut. In 1992, Kristi Yamaguchi captivated audiences with her gold-

Greg Louganis performs a dive during the 1988 Seoul Olympics.

Speed skater Bonnie Blair (left) and figure skater Kristi Yamaguchi (right, at left) won gold medals at the 1992 Winter Games in Albertville.

medal-winning performance in Albertville, France.

Slicing over the ice with fast leg strokes, U.S. speed skater Eric Heiden made victory seem easy at the 1980 Olympics in Lake Placid, New York. Participating in all five speed-skating events, including the 10,000-meter race, Heiden captured the gold each time. Another fine speed skater, Bonnie Blair, won a gold medal at Calgary, Canada, in 1988 and two gold medals at Albertville in 1992.

The 1984 Summer Games in Los Angeles kept Americans glued to their television sets to watch Mary Lou Retton. The spunky sixteen-year-old earned five medals in gymnastics, including the gold in the women's all-around competition. At Barcelona in 1992, gymnast Shannon Miller won five medals, including the silver in the all-around.

Mary Lou Retton

In recent Olympic contests, Carl Lewis has burned up the track in the sprints and taken flight over the long-jump pit. In 1984, Lewis made history by winning the same four Olympic events Jesse Owens won in 1936. His His long-jump victory at Barcelona in 1992 made him the first Olympian to win that event three times.

At Seoul in 1988, Lewis shared the track spotlight with Florence Griffith-Joyner and Jackie Joyner-Kersee, who are sisters-in-law. Fans shouted "Flo-Jo" whenever Griffith-Joyner

Carl Lewis (in center) during the 1988 Summer Games in Seoul

Florence Griffith-Joyner

zoomed down the track. With one silver and three gold medals, the stylish sprinter rightly earned the title of fastest woman in the world. Joyner-Kersee captured gold in the long jump and in the difficult seven-event heptathlon, in spite of a strained knee. With a second heptathlon win in 1992, she became the first woman to win more than one Olympic multi-event competition. That year, Gail Devers's victory in the 100-meter dash had special meaning; the year before, she almost had to have her feet amputated because of complications from a thyroid condition.

A highlight of Barcelona was the gold-medal-

Jackie Joyner-Kersee aims the javelin during the 1988 Seoul Games.

Magic Johnson and Michael Jordan congratulate each other on a good play during the 1992 Summer Games in Barcelona.

winning U.S. men's basketball team. The "Dream Team," touted as the best basketball team ever assembled, included such NBA superstars as Magic Johnson, Michael Jordan, and Larry Bird.

During each Olympiad, the Olympic flag flutters above the Olympic Village. Its five interlocking rings represent the five separate continents joined together in goodwill. The spirit of the modern Olympics fulfills Baron de Coubertin's dream. "The most important thing in the Olympic Games," he once reminded athletes, "is not to win but to take part, just as the most important thing in life is not the triumph but the struggle."

INDEX

PHOTO CREDITS

Cover, 1, Focus on Sports; 2, The Bettmann Archive; 4, Erich Kamper; 5 (top), United States Olympic Committee; 5 (bottom), UPI/Bettmann; 6, 7 (bottom), North Wind; 7 (top), The Bettmann Archive; 8, 9 (top), Missouri Historical Society; 9 (bottom), United States Olympic Committee; 10 (left), Focus on Sports; 10 (right), 11, Sports Chrome East/West; 12 (top), UPI/Bettmann; 12 (bottom), The Bettmann Archive; 13, Historical Pictures/Stock Montage; 14 (both photos), AP/Wide World; 15 (left), UPI/Bettmann; 15 (right), Springer/Bettmann Film Archive; 16, United States Olympic Committee; 17 (both photos), 18 (top), AP/Wide World; 18 (bottom), UPI/Bettmann; 19, United States Olympic Committee; 20, UPI/Bettmann; 21 (both photos), 22, AP/Wide World; 23, United States Olympic Committee; 24 (bottom photos), AP/Wide World; 24 (top), 25 (top), UPI/Bettmann; 25 (bottom), 26 (top), AP/Wide World; 26 (bottom), UPI/Bettmann; 27, Focus on Sports; 28 (left), Sports Chrome East/West; 28 (right), Wide World; 29 (top), AP/Wide World; 29 (bottom), 30, Focus on Sports; 31, AP/Wide World

Picture Identifications:
Cover: Florence Griffith-Joyner competing during the 1984 Los Angeles Games
Page 1: Members of the 1984 U.S. Olympic men's swim team show off their gold medals.
Page 2: Spectators enter the stadium on the opening day of the first modern Olympics.

Project Editor: Shari Joffe
Designer: Karen Yops
Cornerstones of Freedom Logo: David Cunningham

ABOUT THE AUTHOR

Zachary Kent grew up in Little Falls, New Jersey, and received an English degree from St. Lawrence University. Following college, he worked at a New York City literary agency for two years and then began his writing career. To support himself while writing, he has worked as a taxi driver, shipping clerk, and house painter.